THE CHILDREN'S ANTI-VIOLENCE BOOK

DON'T BE A MENACE ON SUNDAYS!

WRITTEN BY
ADOLPH MOSER
Ed.D.

ILLUSTRATED BY
DAVID MELTON

LANDMARK EDITIONS, INC.
P.O. BOX 270169   1402 KANSAS AVENUE KANSAS CITY, MISSOURI 64127

Third Printing

Editorial Coordinator: Nancy R. Thatch
Creative Coordinator: David Melton

Printed in the United States of America

Landmark Editions, Inc.
P.O. Box 270169
1402 Kansas Avenue
Kansas City, Missouri 64127
(816) 241-4919
www.Landmarkeditions.com

I would rather be a friend
than a MENACE!

I would rather be a helper
than a bully!

I would rather be a doctor
than a killer.

I would rather be a builder
than a bomber.

I would rather be a hero
than a violent person.

Violent people hurt others.
Heroes help other people.

Dr. Adolph Moser

It happens every day.

Someone hits someone,

or kicks someone,

or shoots someone.

6

Why do people
do such violent things?

Sometimes
people do violent things
because they want
something that belongs
to another person.

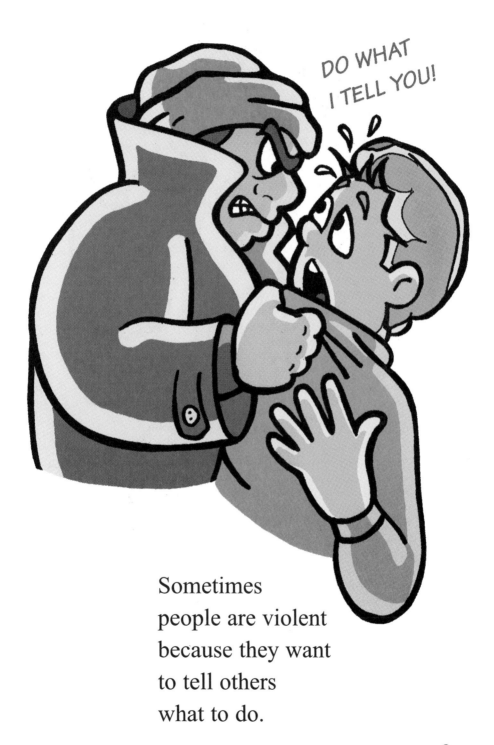

Sometimes
people are violent
because they want
to tell others
what to do.

Sometimes
people become violent
because they are SO ANGRY,
they can't control their actions.

10

Sometimes
people do violent things
because they
want attention.

And sometimes
people start to
act violently
because they have seen

too much violence
on television,
in the movies,
and in video games.

On television, in movies,
and in video games,

14

acts of violence can
look and sound exciting.

Some children think,
  "WOW! Those things look like fun!"

"When I am old enough,
I'm going to get a real fast car."

"I'm going to speed down the road
  and crash into things!"

16

"I'll learn how to fight,
    and I'll hit people and knock them down!"

"I'll get a gun
and learn how to shoot it!"

"And I'll learn how to make bombs
    and blow up buildings!"

17

Some adults think that way, too.

They drive too fast!

They get into fights!

They make bombs!

And they blow up buildings!

19

People who act violently
are not new to the world.
Thousands of years ago,
our ancestors fought
with one another.

The first weapons they used
were the only weapons they had —
    their fists and their feet,
    and sometimes,
    they used their teeth.

21

But, through the years,
people discovered better weapons.
They found —

Rocks were better than fists.

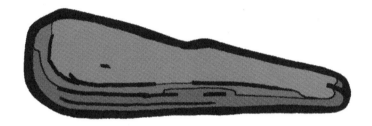

Clubs were better than rocks.

Knives were better than clubs.

Spears were better than knives.

22

Bows and arrows were better than spears.

And then — someone invented a gun.

Guns were easy to use and fast to shoot!
So a lot of people wanted guns.

Knives and spears,
and bows and arrows, and guns
are not good or bad.
They are simply tools.

Guns and spears,
and bows and arrows
are good tools for hunting.
Knives are good tools for
cutting meat and
chopping vegetables.

But some people
use these tools for bad things.

Robbers like to carry guns
so they can steal from others.
They use their guns
to threaten and bully people.
Sometimes they shoot people
and even kill them.

It may be exciting
and fun to watch people
do violent things in movies,
on television, and in video games.

But it is not fun
when suddenly,
you are the one who
is being threatened.

Anyone who
has ever been in
a serious car wreck
knows it is not fun
to be in a wreck.

And anyone who
has ever been hit
and knocked around
knows it is not fun
to be hit or beaten up.

Anyone who has ever
had a gun aimed
at him or her
knows it is not fun
to have a gun aimed
at him or her.

And anyone who
has ever been shot
knows it is not
fun to be shot.

The hitting and the shooting
that are shown in movies
and on television shows are not real.

They are only PRETEND.

The actors don't really hit each other.
They don't really shoot each other.
And they don't really get killed.
They just PRETEND to do these things.

After a movie or TV show
is finished,
the actors are paid,
and they go somewhere else
to make another movie.

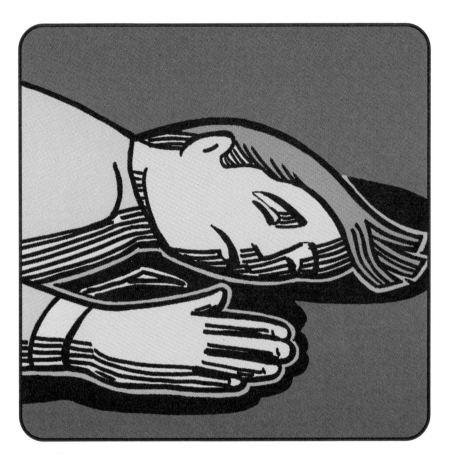

But, in real life
it is not the same.

In real life,
when real people get hurt,
they feel real pain,
and they bleed real blood.
And when real people are killed,
they really die.

Sometimes in movies and on TV,
the people who do violent things
are shown as strong and daring people.
Some kids think, "I want to be like them!"

But, why would anyone want to be like them?

People who hurt others
are bullies and killers.
They are a MENACE
to other people!

Why would anyone
want to be a MENACE
when he or she could be a HERO?

Heroes help other people.

No hero would walk
into a restaurant or a school,
pull out a gun,
and start shooting
at everyone in sight.

Not only do bullies
shoot other people
and kill other people,
they also hurt the families
and friends of the people
they have shot or killed.

When people are shot
or killed,
it makes their friends
and their family members
feel very sad.

The people who
bullies and killers
hurt or kill
are not always adults.
Sometimes the
victims are children!

How could anyone
be proud of
hurting or killing
a little child?

What can you do
to protect yourself from violence
and keep yourself from
becoming a violent person?

You can do a number of things:

1. You can realize that violent people
   are mean and dangerous.
   A violent person can be a MENACE
   to you and to other people.

2. If you know people who enjoy watching violent things and doing violent things, DON'T spend time with them!

Instead — spend time with people who are nice and who enjoy helping others.

People who are violent
often end in violence.
Many of them are shot or killed.

Those who are not killed
are often sent to prisons.
There, they are
locked up in cells,
and they have to
live apart from
their families and friends.

If you do not want to be killed
or spend your life in prison,
STAY AWAY from violent people!

And DON'T ALLOW YOURSELF
to become a violent person.

3. DON'T ALLOW YOURSELF to become fascinated by violence!

4. DON'T WATCH one violent movie or TV show after another!

5. DON'T PLAY violent video games! Find other kinds of shows to watch and other kinds of games to play.

6. DON'T THINK ABOUT
   ways you can hurt people.
   Instead —
   THINK ABOUT WAYS
   you can help others.
   And then — HELP THEM!

7. DON'T PLAY WITH GUNS!

Every year thousands of children
are accidentally shot.
Many children are even killed.

If there is a gun
in your house —
DON'T TOUCH IT!

If you find a gun anywhere —
DON'T SHOW IT
to a friend,
or to a brother or a sister,
or to a schoolmate!

Instead — TELL AN ADULT!

8. If you see anything
that looks like
it may be a bomb,

DON'T PICK IT UP!

DON'T EVEN TOUCH IT!

Get away from it
as fast as you can!
Tell an adult
or telephone the police
IMMEDIATELY!

9. If you learn that a friend,
   or a relative, or a schoolmate
   is carrying a gun or has a bomb,
   tell your parents, or your teacher,
   or a police officer
       IMMEDIATELY!

10. If you hear
a friend or a classmate
talking about
getting a gun,
or making a bomb,
or planning to hurt anyone,

   TELL AN ADULT
      IMMEDIATELY!

You don't want
to become a "snoop"
or a "busybody".

But it is smart
for you to "play it safe"
and to always be alert
to things that are
happening around you.

You are not responsible
for the things
that other people do
or the way they behave.

But you are
responsible
for the things
that you do
and the way
you behave.

Anytime you are upset
and you think
you are about
to become a menace —
STOP!

Tighten one of
your hands into a fist.
Then hold your fist
in front of your face
and look at it.

Take a deep breath.
Then slowly open your fingers.
As your fingers open,
you will start to relax, and . . .

your violent urges will float up
and disappear into the air.

You can release
your urges to be violent
whenever you need to —
    At home. At school.
    Anytime! Anywhere!

You don't want to be a violent person.

Instead —
You want to be kind and friendly.

When you are kind and friendly,
more people will like you.
And you will be a happier person.

THERE ARE SIX OTHER DAYS

42 Pages • Full Color • Hardcover
ISBN 0-933849-18-4

55 Pages • Full Color • Hardcover
ISBN 0-933849-38-9

61 Pages • Full Color • Hardcover
ISBN 0-933849-54-0

In these very informative handbooks for children, Dr. Adolph Moser offers practical approaches and effective techniques that can help young people deal with STRESS, SELF-ESTEEM, ANGER, GRIEF, LYING and their PARENTS DIVORCING.

All six of these Emotional Impact books are highly recommended.

For years, there has been a need for a really good stress-management book for children. Finally, it has occurred in the form of ***Don't Pop Your Cork On Mondays!*** I have seen no other book like it. I enthusiastically recommend it to parents, teachers, clinicians, and children.

— Theodore J. Tollefson, Ph.D., Clinical Psychologist

Read alouds should be entertaining and informative for both children and adults. ***Don't Pop Your Cork On Mondays!*** fits the rule to a tee. Adolph Moser has given parents and children an enjoyable way to learn about their own behavior.

I love it!

— William F. Russell, author of CLASSICS TO READ ALOUD TO YOUR CHILDREN

Every school year should start with having students read ***Don't Feed The Monster On Tuesdays!*** I can't think of a better beginning for children.

Try it. You'll like it!

— Bonnie G. Molloy, Educator, Parent, Nurturing Grandparent

IN THE WEEK — WOW!

The Emotional Impact Series Explains and Informs! They are invaluable resources for clinicians, teachers, parents, and everyone else who works with children.
— Judy S. Freedman, LCSW,
Creator of STRESS*ED,
School Social Worker, and Parent

I highly recommend **Don't Feed The Monster on Tuesdays!** Make a child feel special by reading this book to him or her. It will be fun!
— Robert S. Craig, Ed.D.,
Psychologist and Clinic Director

Don't Rant & Rave On Wednesdays! is a delightful addition to Dr. Moser's Emotional Impact Series! With the right combination of information and humor, he clearly defines the emotion of anger and offers workable suggestions that can help youngsters learn how to control their own behavior.
— Sue Clarke, Coordinator of
Gifted Programs

In **Don't Rant & Rave On Wednesdays!**, Dr. Moser presents clinically accurate, helpful lessons in a most entertaining manner. The examples are well chosen, and the engaging illustrations carry the text into the hearts and minds of children of all ages.
— Dr. Debra E. Taylor-McGee,
HSPP, Licensed Psychologist

YOU'LL WANT TO READ ALL OF THEM!

61 Pages • Full Color • Hardcover
ISBN 0-933849-60-5

61 Pages • Full Color • Hardcover
ISBN 0-933849-76-1

61 Pages • Full Color •Hardcover
ISBN 0-933849-77-X

Adolph Moser — author

Dr. Adolph Moser is a licensed clinical psychologist in private practice, specializing in bio-behavioral and cognitive approaches to stress-related syndromes. He is founder of the Center for Human Potential, a nonprofit organization with holistic focus on preventing acute onsets of stress in children. While Chief Psychologist at the Indiana Youth Center, he implemented a biofeedback laboratory and directed a nine-year research project on the effects of relaxation techniques in the treatment of stress disorders. That study culminated in the development of the nationally distributed stress-management program, entitled SYSTEMATIC RELAXATION TRAINING.

Raised in Indiana, Dr. Moser is a graduate of the universities of Purdue and Indiana. He is certified in biofeedback and is a Diplomate Stressologist. He is also a Diplomate in Behavioral Medicine and Psychotherapy, and a Fellow and Diplomate in Medical Psychotherapy. Dr. Moser is listed in WHO'S WHO IN THE BIO-BEHAVIORAL SCIENCES. In 1987, he received the "Outstanding Psychologist of the Year" award from the National Prisoners' Rights Union.

After becoming parents, Dr. Moser and his wife, Dr. Kathryn Moser, who is also a psychologist, expanded their professional practices to include normal problems of childhood and parenting. They co-authored a newspaper column, "Positive Parenting," for ten years.

Dr. Moser is the father of three children, spanning pre-school to adolescence, which explains his perennial interest in stress and anger management.

All of Dr. Moser's books in his EMOTIONAL IMPACT SERIES have received outstanding reviews and enthusiastic acceptance from children, parents, counselors, and educators nationwide.

David Melton — illustrator

David Melton is one of the most versatile and prolific talents on the literary and art scenes today. His literary works span the gamut of factual prose, news-reporting, analytical essays, magazine articles, features, short stories, and poetry and novels in both the adult and juvenile fields. In the past thirty years, twenty-one of his books have been published. Several of them have been translated into a number of foreign languages.

Mr. Melton has illustrated ten of his own books and seven by other authors. Many of his drawings and paintings have been reproduced as fine art prints, posters, puzzles, calendars, book jackets, record covers, mobiles, and note cards, and have been featured in national publications.

Since a number of Mr. Melton's books are enjoyed by children, he has visited hundreds of schools throughout the country as a principal speaker in Young Authors' Days, Author-in-Residence Programs, and Children's Literature Festivals. Each year, he also conducts his WRITTEN & ILLUSTRATED BY... WORKSHOPS for students and educators, effectively teaching participants to write and illustrate original books.

Mr. Melton's teacher's manual, WRITTEN & ILLUSTRATED BY..., has been highly acclaimed and has been used by thousands of teachers nationwide to instruct their students in how to write and illustrate amazing books.

Mr. Melton is also a book publisher. During the last fourteen years, as Creative Coordinator at Landmark Editions, he has supervised the publication of more than fifty books by other authors and illustrators.